David Picken

Poems and Songs

With a Memoir of the Author, and Notes

David Picken

Poems and Songs
With a Memoir of the Author, and Notes

ISBN/EAN: 9783744770620

Printed in Europe, USA, Canada, Australia, Japan

Cover: Foto ©Thomas Meinert / pixelio.de

More available books at **www.hansebooks.com**

POEMS AND SONGS

BY THE LATE

DAVID PICKEN.

PREFACE.

THE present Volume, as is elsewhere explained, has been issued in compliance with the request of a numerous circle of friends of the late DAVID PICKEN. The Committee who have taken charge of the publication have to express their thanks to the gentleman who has kindly edited the Volume and furnished the Memoir and Notes. They feel confident that those interested will be satisfied that the work has been accomplished in a proper spirit, and in such a way as to be a fitting memorial of a friend they all so much esteemed.

PAISLEY, *August, 1875.*

CONTENTS.

	PAGE
PREFACE,	v.
CONTENTS,	vii.
MEMOIR,	1–16

POEMS.

Kilmalcolm; our Club's first trip thereto,	17
Kilmalcolm re-visited by the Club,	21
A Dream,	27
The Teachings of a Winter's Day,	31
A Lay Sermon,	33
The Go-a-heads,	37
Sabbath Morning Reflections,	41
To the Memory of Allan Stewart,	43
Epistle to a Friend,	45
On the Death of Janet Picken,	47
To a Tract about to be posted to a distant friend,	48
Farewell to James Ronald,	49
To the Memory of James Picken,	51
The Weaver's Child,	53
Storie Street Well,	55
The Ghaist o' Storie Street Well,	60

CONTENTS.

	PAGE
Fragment: Epistle to a Friend,	64
The Martyrs' Grave,	67
Elegy on Walter Peacock,	69
Alas! they're gone who cheered me,	73
On reading a Burlesque Sermon to Bachelors,	74
A Light to Lighten those who leaped into Political Darkness,	75
School Board Elections and Comic Cartoons,	78
Fragment: Dear S——,	81
The School Board and the Drill Hall Indignation Meeting,	82
The Tannahill Centenary,	86
Free Breakfasts and Bonded Lights,	91
Whigs and Tories,	92
Tom Hood in a fix,	95
The New Year Expectant,	96
To Sanct Crispin,	96
Fragment,	97

SONGS.

The Gallant Paisley Weaver,	99
When you and I, Jeannie,	103
Wac's me,	104
"Heart's-Ease,"	106

MEMOIR.

DAVID PICKEN, the author of the modest effusions contained in the present volume, was born at 37 Storie Street, Paisley, on the 16th of April, 1809, just at the time when that love of song for which his native town has acquired a certain celebrity was at its height. Mr. PICKEN's family belonged to the then extensively-spread local industry of hand-loom weaving which, in its finer departments of silk and gauze, was a light, cheerful occupation, combining ample remuneration for labour with an amount of spare time that gave opportunities for cultivating that love of nature which, in the case of Robert Tannahill, Robert Allan, and numbers of their compeers, welled out into pleasing and graceful song. To the loom Mr. PICKEN remained attached through life, sharing contentedly its varying fortunes, and enjoying to the last that pride in his occupation to which he has given vent so fully in his song of "The gallant Paisley Weaver." Sprung from a respectable household, he received the customary round of education then deemed sufficient. The curriculum of study in the schools of that period was by no means so extended as at present; but whether from the soundness of the teaching, as far as it went, or the habits of after reading and reflection engrafted during their limited course of tuition, men of Mr. PICKEN's stamp may be satisfactorily adduced as examples of how effectively they could keep their ground with those who, in more recent times, have enjoyed, presumably at least, so many more favourable opportunities of culture.* In the times of his boyhood, reading, writing, and arithmetic were all that was taught in the ordinary schools to which tradesmen sent their children. The work was simple and soon got over, and but a few "quarters" were deemed necessary to get all that was required. Where day education had from family necessities been cut short, any hiatus left was filled up by the opportunities of the "night school." The Shorter Catechism and the grand old lessons of Bible history, with some collection or other of standard specimens of English Literature, were about all that was put into the hands of the children; and yet what Burns says of the physical upbringing of the Scottish peasantry may be said also of their intellectual training,—

"buirdly chiels and clever hizzies
Were bred on sic a fare as this is."

Of the period Mr. PICKEN remained at school we have no particular record. It was probably not a lengthened one; but whatever amount of intellectual culture he there received was afterwards amplified and improved by reading and observation. His boy-

---

* Mr. PICKEN, it may be mentioned, was nephew to the well-known Andrew Picken, author of the "Dominie's Legacy," "Traditionary Stories of the West of Scotland," "The Black Watch," &c., who, after leaving Paisley, occupied a distinguished position in the literary circles of London.

hood, it must be remembered, was a time of more than usual excitement and inquiry, especially in political matters. He was but entering on his seventh year when the return of the first French Emperor from Elba and the "Hundred Days" that ended for him so disastrously at Waterloo were occupying the attention of all classes, and of none more so than the artizans of Paisley, who, during the preceding twenty years, had been famous for their interest in the stirring events of continental history. Regarding the French Revolution as the overthrow of "Despotism" and the establishment of the principle of Right over that of Might, the "Blacknebs," as they were called, of Paisley were not without a certain sympathy for the fallen Emperor, and had their fears that his overthrow might tend to the retardment of healthy political progress at home. It was the habit, of the weaving class especially, to discuss freely at street corners and by "loom-stoops" the events of the time, and their "draw-boy" assistants hearing all these discussions, necessarily soon became quite as ardent politicians as their masters. The five years immediately succeeding Waterloo were years of great excitement amongst the working classes. The "Peace" to which they had longingly looked as likely to bring almost millenial blessings, had, as far as employment and remuneration were concerned, results almost diametrically opposite; the spirit of discontent spread itself on every hand, and the desire for political amelioration and sweeping changes of our representative system became deep-seated and popular. The repressive spirit displayed by the Government led to extravagant notions of resistance on the part of the people, till at last the agitation ended in the disasters of 1819 and '20, when James Wilson at Glasgow, and Baird and Hardie at Stirling, suffered death by the hands of the public executioner, and James Spiers at Paisley fortuitously escaped the same fate, through the statute under which he had been exceptionally tried to make conviction more certain requiring a *unanimous* verdict. In the discussions of this eventful period, DAVID PICKEN, boy as he was, was doubtless interested, and the political leanings then engendered adhered to him through life. Of the local political excitement of 1819-20 he must have had vivid recollections. The immediate neighbourhood of his family's residence was that of two of the more remarkable incidents of the "Radical time;" as within a hundred yards or so of it stood both the then newly-erected St. George's Church, in which James Speirs was tried, and the Methodist Chapel whose railings were torn down by the populace, in their frenzy, to serve as weapons of attack or defence. At the age he then was, it is more than probable that DAVID PICKEN was an eye-witness on both occasions, and had the seeds sown of that sympathy with the Reformers of the time that led him long afterwards to regard their movements as

" the last embattled stroke
That Scotchmen struck at vile oppression's yoke;"

but wherein, alas,

" they found their enterprise
Was circumvented and betrayed by spies."

In the movements for Parliamentary Reform which,

beginning in 1829, gathered into irresistible strength after the French Revolution of 1830, and eventually culminated in the great Parliamentary concessions of 1832, Mr. PICKEN continued the warm and steadfast friend of political progress. Several of his pieces refer to this and immediately succeeding periods, and give expression to the dissatisfaction of the great bulk of the working classes at the pusillanimous if not treacherous conduct of the Whig Party, who, finding themselves at length in power, displayed no alacrity to push on still further the enfranchisement of the people, but evidenced a desire rather to "rest and be thankfu'," in the secret belief, doubtless, that having had their immediate political cravings gratified, they might travel farther and fare worse. This policy, which finally brought on the Chartist agitations of 1839-40-41, alienated from them the sympathies of the working class, and of no one more than Mr. PICKEN, who regarded every popular advance in the most favourable of lights, and the special gratification of whose later years must have been that he had lived to see that full, fair, and free enfranchisement of the people that he, in common with his class, had so long desiderated.

Throughout life Mr. PICKEN thus stood manfully by his order. With the interests of working men his best feelings were intertwined; and although his modest and retiring character led him to shrink from any ostentatious intermeddling with social questions and to confine his expressions of opinion to simple conversation or an occasional outpouring in verse,—wrathful or humorous as best fitted his mood,—still, that his interest in such topics was keen and abiding there is ample evidence in the present volume to show; and whether it might be reprehensible excess in trading speculations, undue manifestations of selfishness of class against class, the withholding of popular rights, the misreadings of public calamities, the unseemly witticisms of political contests, or the stinginess that would mar liberality where the interests of the young were at stake, he had not only his opinion, but the courage to express it. It may be that occasionally he wrote quite as much from his feelings of the moment as from his cooler judgment. Of this he was himself perfectly aware.

> " Alack-a-day, that my *impulsive* muse
> Should for herself choose such ungracious subject,
> Knowing, as she does well, the Press refuse
> Insertion to such samples of her budget.
> Still, she cries out to *propagate* her views,
> And *I unto her wayward whims am subject*."

He had all the workman's detestation of the "tricks of trade," and was wont to ascribe its periodical depressions to the rapacities of the wages-breaker and overproducer.

> " Of late there have been Achans in our camps,
> Whose selfish lust for the unrighteous mammon
> Has spread distrust through our commercial ranks,
> And rendered trade a wicked game of gammon.
> Had these with Joshua been on Jordan's banks,
> They'd have been stoned, or hung as high as Haman.
> In trade or war, when men commence to plunder,
> Society and armies fall asunder."

His ideas were, that trade ought to be conducted on

principles less selfish and more philanthropic. He could not understand how, when

> "God's mercy had provided
> In barn and byre an ample store,—
> Enough to spread, *if right divided,*
> The family board of rich and poor,
> That yet, despite this great profusion,
> The poor repine and cry for bread;"

and held by

> "the new Gospel plan,
> Of doing as we would that others
> In like way should do to us;
> In works of love serving each other,
> As we or they are prosperous;"

as well as by the assurance that

> "to love thy neighbour
> As thou would'st thine own dear self,
> Would add a blessing on man's labour,
> And guard against unrighteous pelf."

Such sentiments the more critical may be inclined to characterise as vague and hazy, and to set them down as crudities that a more intimate contact and personal intermixing in the great battle of life would have modified or dissipated. Be it so. It was perhaps the good fortune of Mr. PICKEN that he remained in a sphere where the chicaneries of the great world and the occasional meannesses and peccadillos of commerce had no opportunity to strike root or grow.

That there was a deep-seated feeling of veneration for religious things in the character of Mr. PICKEN, is evident from the general tenor of his verses. His detestation of such

> "humbug, as that our dull trade woes
> Are to be regarded as God's visitation;"

or of such assertions as that

> "the chiefest sinners were the working classes,
> For 'twas their special food had turned to dust and ashes;"

or the opinion

> "that a formal prayer's omission
> Does not entail upon our temporal state
> Those ills that surely follow crime's commission,"

is not to be viewed as indicative of any spirit of irreverence. Such pieces as "The Dream," where his

> "Sainted sister, child of Heaven,
> She whom subtle death had driven
> From this sad and changing shore,"

comes again to revisit him and listen to his enquiries why she had left "her home in glory,"—that on the memory of his brother,—his "Sabbath Morning Reflections,"—and one or two others, are alike indicative of his susceptibility to solemn and even religious emotions.

Of his humanity and kindly interest in "all that breathes," we have ample evidence. Of the poor man's child he could say—

> "God help thee, child; with hardships *soon*
> *Thou hast become acquaint;*"

while amidst his delineations of a winter's day, the kind considerations for even the humbler orders of the animal creation that welled up in the bosom of the great high priest of Scottish song, when he turned up the nest of the field-mouse with his ploughshare, were not wanting in that of his more humbly-gifted brother,—

" On northern blasts, the snow-flakes flicker
    Wi' freezing sough across the lea ;
The birds upon the hedges twitter,
    Wi' drooping wing and closing e'e.

Poor little things, though Winter rages
    An' fields are covered o'er wi' snaw,
'Neath bramble, brake, or sheltered hedges,
    They pick up food unseen by a'."

The retiring modesty of Mr. PICKEN was another strong feature of his character. He never thrust himself to the front, and rarely obtruded his poetical effusions upon public notice. His gifts were known only to a select circle of friends, and that circle he displayed no anxiety to enlarge. Still, he was inclined to sociality and innocent mirth, and never allowed any diversity of fortune between himself and early friends to lower in the slightest his self-respect. Amidst, he assures us,

" the changes of my passing years,
I still have friends congenial and true ;
    Although we move in various trading spheres,
We often meet and have a glass or two,
And talk on general subjects old and new."

His pursuit of the muse, too, was of the most unworldly and unselfish kind. His exercise of verse was an enjoyment in which he indulged for its own exceeding great reward; and the solace he enjoyed from it sweetened considerably his quiet and retired life. The circle of his " Club " was congenial and inviting, and within its limited round he appeared to find enough of social intercourse to satisfy his wants.

Mr. PICKEN remained throughout life a bachelor, and resided in family with his father till the death of the latter, about 1853. He then removed from his much-loved Storie Street to 12 Stevenson Street, where he eventually died. Whether his prolonged celibacy resulted from some early slight is not to be gathered from his writings, although an expression in one of his impromptus would almost lead to such a supposition. "The impression," he says,

> " of an early love will cling
> Unto the heart until the head grows hoary.
> Nay, many instances I could easily bring,
> Alike from ancient and from modern story,
> Of dying men who even spoke with gladness
> Of meeting soon the cause of their long earthly sadness."

Be the fact in his case as it may, the attentions and comforts enjoyed with a branch of the family sufficed for his requirements, and he enjoyed the *abandon* and freedom that celibacy unquestionably affords. His attachments were entirely local. Little from home, his affections entwined themselves around the scenes and associates he had been familiar with from childhood. The old pump, where he had played — and where perhaps "Auld Tam had gien his lugs a clinking," —"Wattie Pe'ock," at whose drum he'd "flung a stane, to gar it soun'," —"Gleniffer's Wood and Glen," "Inchinnan Loan," and "the old Douglas trees," — all of which are more or less alluded to, prove this locality of feeling, and show the unpretending simplicity of his character.

During the summer and autumn of 1874, evidences of declining strength began to manifest themselves to his friends. Of this, there is evidence enough, he had for a time been personally conscious. Three years previously he had said,—

" I find the tottering of my footfall paces
  Requires a staff to keep me straight and staid ; "

whilst, on the occasion of last year's centenary celebration of the birth of Tannahill, he expresses his desire, in the company of his "quaint descriptive muse," to *wander* up the hill and *read* the descriptions of the rejoicings.

" 'Twill make my bosom thrill
With the warm glow of brighter, younger years ;
For now I'm old, and could not *press* uphill,
To join the throng and hear their joyous cheers."

The end at length came. About the beginning of December he caught a severe cold, resulting in an illness of several weeks, and terminating in an attack of pulmonary congestion, to which he succumbed on Sunday, 3rd January. On the Wednesday following, his remains were deposited in the family lair in the Highchurch burying-ground, in the presence of about a hundred gentlemen representing all classes in the community.

" One morn we missed him on the accustomed hill,
  Along the heath, and near his favourite tree ;
  Another came,—nor yet beside the rill,
  Nor up the lawn, nor at the wood was he."

Thus ended a life so quiet and unobtrusive in its character and so uneventful and unchequered, as to afford little scope for extended remark. The round of daily duty had been too uniform and unvaried, and too faithfully and steadily performed, to give that light and shade which constitute the charm of all records of individual or national character. Of such men as DAVID PICKEN, it may be truly said that "they pass their lives obscure" till some accidental circumstance "drags them into fame;" and of such too it must be confessed, despite intellectual worth and homely virtues, that on their memorial tablets, too often, "their name, their years, the place of fame and elegy supply." Little known beyond their immediate circles, they "are soon forgotten when they're gone," unless where, as in the present instance, the hands of loving friends gather together memorials that, but for such care, might have been soon hopelessly lost or scattered. If "even in our ashes live our wonted fires," the modest collection of literary remains here published will bring back, not unfrequently, recollections of its author, and keep his remembrance green in the memories of those at least who enjoyed his friendship.

In the preceding remarks, necessarily more biogaphical than critical, Mr. PICKEN has been-referred to rather as a man and a politician than as a poet; still, although the tenets of his political and social creed were soundly honest, and his spirit of philanthropy undoubted, it will be as the quiet and observant humourist, the genial appreciator and delineator of natural scenery and homely character, and the weaver of quaint and peculiar verse, that he will be most lovingly remembered. There need be no desire to set him high amongst the gifted sons of song; his own modesty would have spurned any such idea. A place among the Minor Bards of his *County* is all his admirers claim, feeling confident that with such a position he would have been more than content. That he possessed a creditable amount of poetic genius few will deny; he had that fine appreciation of nature's beauties that none but poetic minds possess, and that gift of word-painting that not only conveys accurate impressions of the things seen, but of the thoughts to which they give rise and with which they remain associated, which is characteristic of the poetic temperament. No better example of his keen and accurate observation, racy power of description, and blend of quaint humour, can be given than some of the stanzas on "Kilma'com." First, his description of the irregularly-formed village—

" Kilmalcolm is a *grotesque* little town—
   House walls of earthstone, roofs of heather thack;
   No plan of street or road has been laid down,—
   One cannot tell the front-door from the back!

    .   .   .   .   .   .

" 'Out of the world and into Kilma'com'
   Is often quoted when one's pressed with care;
For 'tis, forsooth, a rural catacomb,
   Where lies, *embalmed* in *heather-scented* air,
   A *labyrinthian range* or *crooked lair*
Of houses, built with no commercial view;
   The natives *till* the ground,—*no trade is there,—*
They pass their lives as Scotchmen wont to do,
Content with *parritch*, a *Scotch plaid*, and *bonnet blue*."

And then his delineation of the face of nature on the wintry day of his second visit,—

> " We took our former path down Glenburn side,
>   Then o'er the moor amang the *snow-clad* heather;
>   See, see my town-bred muse try to describe
>   This country scene of stern, *mid-winter weather;*
>   The floating clouds *unveil the sky-blue ether,*
>   The sunbeams and the gleams of *unsoiled* snow
>   *Meet, blush, embrace,* and *dance* together;
>   Anon a heavy cloud, with *gloomy brow,*
>   Does *pall* the beauties of the panoramic show.

> " Where are the farmer's landmarks, where his field
>   Of winter wheat or cattle-grazing park?
>   Marshes and lochs, *by ice and snow concealed,*
>   Have lost the ripple of the water-mark;
>   All things are swaddled in a sleeping sark
>   Of *such unspotted purity and brightness,*
>   Imagination, dazzled, gropes in the dark
>   To find a simile or a proper likeness;
>   *Celestial purity alone* excels the scene in *whiteness.*"

The verses on Storie Street Well are admirable specimens of his quiet, pawky humour that could hit off the eccentricities of individual character, without in any way giving offence. The sketch of the old pump in its pristine days, to those who can throw their recollections back for forty or five-and-forty years, must have a charm that, to those who cannot, is perfectly indescribable. The old worthies who took charge, and the long array of expecting recipients in the seasons of summer droughts, all rise up again as they did "lang syne," and shadows of the "arabs" from Rope-a-ree Close and Goose-dubs again throw themselves upon the scene. The description of Tam, "in the same claise he wore langsyne," is particularly graphic. He is pourtrayed as faithfully as if some of the old quaint Dutch painters had done the work, and could he but be transferred to canvass in all the integrity with which the poet has put him on paper, the picture would be a valuable depiction of a "Character." How naively the old *déshabillé* is hit off:—

> "Green worsted apron, *tied wi' string;*
> Blue bonnet, wi' a *checkered* ring;
> His braces o'er his breeks hing slack,—
> See, ane is dangling at his back;
> His stockings *slobber o'er his kuits*,
> Shod wi' a pair o' *bauchelled* boots;"

while, best joke of all, and quite illustrative in its way of the author's keen appreciation of the humourous,—

> "—— ludicrous and strange phisog—
> His mouth is thrawn maist to his lug!
> (A warning taught our early youth,
> *That horrid swearing thrawed his mouth.*)"

Not less happy are the allusions as to the selling of the well,—

> "Na, na, let it stand; it is still of some use
> *E'en to those who would sell it;* when drapping the booze
> They kneel to its pump and say in to themsel'—
> '*It aye comes to water frae Storie Street Well.*'"

In the persual of the volume the reader will find for himself many stray lines indicative of the qualities of mind referred to.

> "Dark vaporous clouds *roll o'er the distant hills*,
> Portentous of a coming shower of rain;"

" The clouded sun *sank* in the *evening shade*,
    That *lay* upon the *far out-stretching seas;* "

" The *gloom* of night was *gathering on the sea ;* "

" The sun along the south horizon
    Wades through dull clouds of misty grey ; "

and many others, might be quoted as examples of how the varying phases of external nature were photographed on his mind, and how happily he could convey his impressions to others.

The present volume appears in compliance with the expressed desire of a numerous circle of friends. Its preparation has been quite a labour of love to those who have taken an interest in it. Unfortunately, like all posthumous publications, it lacks the advantage of personal revision by the author, and this is all the more to be regretted that his papers do not appear to have undergone any special correction with a view to publication. Possibly there may be omissions, but every care has been taken to make the present collection as complete as possible; and as the main design of publication has been to place in the hands of friends a fitting memorial of Mr. PICKEN, it is fondly hoped that that object is now satisfactorily accomplished.

PAISLEY, *August, 1875.*

POEMS AND SONGS.

KILMALCOLM.*

OUR CLUB'S FIRST TRIP THERETO.

THOU sweet mnemonic retrospective muse,
    I know not if thou'rt classed amongst the nine,
But Scotchmen, when they meet for blythe carouse,
    Invoke thee by the name of "Auld Langsyne."
So hand-in-hand we will together join
To dictate these commemorative lays
    Of our Club's trip down the new Greenock line
To where it burrows through Kilmalcolm Braes,
Where we spent one of our bright New-Year holidays.

---

* Long one of the most delightfully rural villages of the County of Renfrew. Situated high up in a moorland district, and apart from the great lines of communication, it had few relations with the "outer world," and might indeed have been described as a region

    "Where every sound was lulled
  To slumber, save the trickling of the rill,
  Or bleat of lamb, or hovering falcon's cry."

But things are now greatly changed, and "out of the world

Kilmalcolm is a *grot*esque little town,—
   House-walls of earthstones, roofs of heather
      thack;
No plan of street or road has been laid down;
   One cannot tell the front door from the back;
   Its founder must have been some old earthquack,
That gave the hills a strong volcanic dose,
   Which time fomented, till their sides did crack
And threw black boulders down to Glenburn moss,
And thus the town of Kilma'com arose.

This may be thought a shocking pun in rhyme,
   Where earthquack acts like to a quack M.D.;
But I am sure the figure's more sublime
   Than the effects of untaught Pharmacy;
   Besides, our Club requires a short essay
On this their first trip of the new-born year;

---

and into Kilma'com" is no longer a proverb. The "new Greenock line" has opened up alike the village and its surroundings; and its pure and bracing air is tempting many denizens of the city to settle down in ornamental villas, now rapidly rising in this formerly-isolated district. A new Inn provides comforts for the casual traveller, and few better day "outs" than Kilma'colm could be afforded for the genial Club with which Mr. Picken was connected, to celebrate its New-Year, or any other holiday.

I know their taste, and will be bold to say,
Although my diction be both quaint and queer,
'Twill please them better than the *Scottish
    Gazetteer.**

"Out of the world and into Kilma'com"
  Is often quoted when one's pressed with care;
For 'tis forsooth a rural catacomb,
  Where lies, embalmed in heather-scented air,
  A labyrinthian range or crooked lair
Of houses, built with no commercial view:
  The natives till the ground,—no trade is there,—
They pass their lives as Scotchmen wont to do,
Content with parritch, a Scotch plaid, and bonnet
    blue.

One of our party acted as our guide,—
  From early boyhood he had known the place;
Another had the forethought to provide
  Some carnal comforts in a travelling case,
  Of which we all partook with thankful grace,
Then rambled as our various fancies led;

---

* *i.e.*, The description of the village in that publication.

Some scanned the Glenburn's bracken-fring'd
    brae-face,
Some look'd for golden quartz down in its bed;
When lo! a shower of hail blew overhead,
Which made us seek the nearest hostelery's shade.

I'll not report our Club's glorification,
    Nor after-dinner speeches in the Inn,
In these my notes on our New-Year ovation;
    To mention names might be a personal sin.
But down in *Peter's** ample proof was seen,
On Eighteen-Seventy's fourth Januar' eve,
    That none of us with drink were lame or blin',
And on each breast you also would perceive
Our incorporation badge—a Kilma'com fern-leaf.

    Jan., 1870.

---

* The Paisley rendezvous of the Club, where the excursionists reassembled after their return to town.

KILMALCOLM RE-VISITED BY THE CLUB.

WITHIN the borough of old Paisley town
    My parents reared me in their fond embraces;
Now threescore fleeting years have o'er me flown,
    And they are long since in their resting-places;
    And many other old familiar faces
I miss at morn or evening promenade.
    I find the tottering of my foot-fall paces
Requires a staff to keep me straight and staid:
Thus all things earthly—Steeples even—topple
    o'er and fade.*

The old familiar sounds I used to hear
    In streets where quiet weavers wont to dwell,—
The family voice, subdued with Godly fear,
    In meek devotion's modulated swell,—

---

* Shortly previous, the old Cross Steeple, one of the most prized of our local landmarks, that stood at the corner of Moss-street and High-street, after having, in consequence of certain "leanings" southwards, been propped for a considerable period, was finally removed.

Is now changed to a foreign drunken yell,
Such as we read of at an Irish fair:
Even when the solemn Sabbath-morning bell
Proclaims the hour for congregated prayer,
Harsh oaths grate through the Scottish silence of
   the Sabbath air.

This is a change which all good men deplore.
   And, searching for its cause, I recollect
Strong drink was cheaper in those days of yore,
   When men had for the Sabbath more respect,—
   I know that parties will to this object;
So, lest my verses should become uncivil,
   I'll only say that I do much suspect
The cause of all this Sabbath-breaking evil
Was at Port-Patrick first imported by the devil.*

Amidst the changes of my passing years,
   I still have friends congenial and true;
Although we move in various trading spheres,
   We often meet and have a glass or two,

---

* The advent of the Irish element by the old route—prior to the introduction of steam communication with the sister isle.

And talk on general subjects old and new,
Until eleven o'clock puts us in min'
    Of Scotland's intolerant curfew,*
Imposed by men who cannot well define
Their stomach's modicum, and therefore measure
    mine.

The germ or nucleus of our Club's formation
    Commenced in *Peter's*, thirty years ago,
Without programme or formal preparation,—
    Good fellowship's the rule to which we bow.
    Our landlord has the power and tact to know
How to keep good company as well as liquor;
    But language fails his management to show
In proper phrase and rightly-sounding metre,
Therefore, I will but say our landlord's name is
    Peter.

We have a mythic claim to Kilma'com,—
    Our club, I mean, and not the muse or I;
A member holds in it, his childhood's home—
    A house, a back-court, and a croft for kye.

---

* The Forbes Mackenzie Act.

The railway station has made feus so high,
He now talks of his ancestral renown,
  And swears that cash will never buy
The claims he has on that famed ancient town,
Named after one of Scotland's chiefs who wore
    the crown.

This ardent love for home long may he cherish!
  The members of the club do not regret
Their annual visit to his native parish,
  To mark Time's changes on his country seat;
  Which stands now in a ruined, falling state,
Of moss-grown grandeur and rank-weed decay;—
  But as our club has had some talk of late
An artist to employ, I think I may
Let photograph or painter's sketch portray
The rural aspect of this wondrous "*propertay.*"

We took our former path down Glenburn side,
  Then o'er the moor amang the snow-clad
    heather;
See, see my town-bred muse try to describe
  This country scene of stern mid-winter weather;
  The floating clouds unveil the sky-blue ether,

The sunbeams and the gleams of unsoiled snow
    Meet, blush, embrace, and dance together;
Anon a heavy cloud, with gloomy brow,
Does pall the beauties of the panoramic show.

Where are the farmer's land-marks, where his field
    Of winter wheat, or cattle-grazing park?
Marshes and lochs, by ice and snow concealed,
    Have lost the ripple of their water-mark;
    All things are swaddled in a sleepin' sark
Of such unspotted purity and brightness,
    Imagination, dazzled, gropes in the dark
To find a simile or a proper likeness,—
Celestial purity alone excels the scene in whiteness.

Dark vaporous clouds roll o'er the distant hills,
    Portentous of a coming shower of rain;
We wend our way where smugglers hid their stills,
    Back to the town of Kilma'com again.
    After refreshment we could not restrain
The feeling to extend our winter trips,
    So we resolved to go to Greenock in the train;
And, after some responsive hurrah, hips!
We all with one accord went down to see the ships.

We walked along the new-formed esplanade,
  Enjoyed the freshness of the ocean's breeze;
The clouded sun sank in the evening shade,
  That lay upon the far out-stretching seas.
  We took the round of several docks and quays,
To inspect the various forms of shipping craft,
  Which lay abreast in twos and threes.
One of us knew their features, fore and aft,
From weather pennon's tall slim-tapered shaft,
Down to the deep-sunk keel's cut water-marked
    draught.

The gloom of night was gathering on the sea,
  So I must finish up my annual lay.
Talking of home, we left the Greenock quay,
  When one into an hôtel led the way,
  Where we had something from a covered tray
By far more savoury than a buttered toast;
  When done, we had another hip, hurrah!
Then, seated in the train, for home we post,
Well pleased with our mid-winter trip through
    snow and biting frost.

January 23, 1871.

A DREAM.

WHILST on my couch of rest reclining,
 With my inmost thoughts defining
  Hardships that were still in store,
Sleep came o'er my senses stealing;
I dreamt, and, oh, a happy feeling—
Yes, a sweet and heavenly feeling—
  Filled my bosom's inmost core.
Surely, thought I, this is pleasure
  That I never felt before.

Methought that I sat lonely, musing—
The moon her pale rays was diffusing
  Light where darkness reigned before—
When suddenly my ear was filled
With sounds as of one deeply skilled—
With sounds as of one deeply skilled—
  In music's sweet enchanting lore;
I leant my head in heart-felt gladness,
  And sought the mystery to explore.

Still I thought the sound came nearer,
The music sounded sweeter, clearer;
    But of earth no tinge it bore.
Surely, thought I, some one enters:
Ah! 'tis some listener who ventures—
Some enchanted one who ventures—
    In at my unbolted door.
Yet I heedless sat and listened,
    With keener relish than before.

The music ceased; I gazed around me;
A happy silence did surround me:
    My heart with joy was brimming o'er.
When, lo, in my enraptured vision
I plainly saw 'twas no delusion—
No; no heartless, vain delusion
    That my cherished fancy bore;
But the form of that dear Sister,
    Whose loss I did so much deplore.

As of old she stood before me,
Then lovingly she bended o'er me,
    Whilst my hair she plaited o'er
With flowers of fair and heavenly blossom.

I sought to clasp her to my bosom—
To this fond, but mortal bosom,
    Sought to clasp her as of yore;
But my arms refused to aid me,
    They my wish seemed to ignore.

I spake, and said with deep emotion,
Yet with reverent devotion,
    Tell me, sister, I implore,
Why hast thou left thy home in glory?
Is it to tell some heavenly story—
To tell me of some heavenly story—
    That's happened on its golden shore?
If so, gentle sister, tell me!—
    She only smiled, but nothing more.

Sainted sister, child of Heaven,
Thou whom subtle death has driven
    From this sad and changing shore,
Tell me hath our Saviour dear, thee
Sent on earth again to cheer me—
To soothe me as of old and cheer me,
    'Midst its never ceasing roar?
Methought she smiled at this, and answered—
    No, brother; never, never more.

Sainted sister, child of Heaven,
Thou whom subtle death has driven
    From this ever changing shore,
Do the friends who lived in union
Here on earth now hold communion—
Hold a lasting, sweet communion
    With the God they did adore?
Methought she smiled at this, and answered—
    They do, and will for evermore.

Then she made as if to leave me;
Stay, sister, said I, I'll not grieve thee
    With my questions any more.
But my request she heard unheeded,
Although with energy I pleaded—
Yea, with heart and soul I pleaded;
    Yet slowly from my sight she wore,
And in a haze of brightness vanished:
    'Twas a dream—and nothing more!

THE TEACHINGS OF A WINTER'S DAY.

THE sun along the south horizon
    Wades through dull clouds of misty grey;
His feeble light is scarce sufficing
    To cheer the gleam of Winter's day.

On northern blasts, the snow-flakes flicker
    Wi' freezing sough across the lea;
The birds upon the hedges twitter,
    Wi' drooping wing and closing e'e.

Poor little things, though Winter rages
    An' fields are covered o'er wi' snaw,
'Neath bramble, brake, or sheltered hedges,
    They pick up food unseen by a'.

Unerring instinct warned the swallow
    To leave these cold, inclement skies;
In southern climes he holds gay gala,
    And feeds upon the sun-born flies.

Other tribes, by hunger driven,
    Leave the inland for the coast,
And there they find that bounteous heaven
    Provides them food untouched by frost.

Thus for the birds that plough nor sow not,
    Neither reap nor build a barn,
The Lord provides; mankind to show that
    From such great teachings they may learn

Of His kind and heavenly care for
    The welfare and support of man:
He knows our wants, and bids us therefore
    Practise the New Gospel plan

Of doing as we would that others,
    In like ways, should do to us;
In works of love serving each other,
    As we or they are prosperous.

A LAY SERMON.

WRITTEN DURING ONE OF THE FORMERLY PERIODIC STAGNATIONS OF THE WEAVING TRADE.

IN case my preface should be deemed verbose,
    I'll leap at once into my meditation
On such humbug as that our dull-trade woes
    Are to be regarded as God's visitation.
I marvel that the clergy don't propose
    A day of fasting and humiliation,
As they did when potatoe crops were fusted;—
We're now much worse, when porridge-pots are
    rusted.

I recollect, when the potatoe blight
    Engaged the energies of man's invention,
To trace its cause by scientific light,
    The clergy, by their timely intervention,
Put all such wicked theories to flight;
    A judgment 'twas, they said, sent with intention
Of showing all and sundry wicked sinners,
That they should say a grace before their dinners.

The people stammered at the startling truth
  Of what their pastors on the fast-day told them:
'Twas a bad habit they had learned in youth,
  Of snatching "tauties"* ere the grace had cooled them,
Puffing and tossing them from hand to mouth;
  For which their pious mothers oft did scold them;
And that the chiefest sinners were the working classes,
For 'twas their special food had turned to dust and ashes.

"Some sins themselves"—I'll quote the question quite—
  "By reason of their several aggravations,
"Are still more heinous in the Holy sight
  "Of God than others," that have palliations;
Meaning (if that I understand aright
  The Book that guides our Sabbath meditations)
That sins of less or more impiety
Are known by their effects upon society.

---

* Potatoes.

Were I a preacher I might here dilate
   On the degrees of sinful man's transgression;
But as I am not, I merely beg to state
   The opinion that a formal prayer's omission
Does not entail upon our temporal state
   Those ills that surely follow crime's commission;
No good we'll get attending Church on Sunday,
If we commence deceit and guile on Monday.

Of late there have been Achans in our camps,
   Whose selfish lust for the unrighteous mammon
Has spread distrust through our commercial ranks,
   And rendered trade a wicked game of gammon.
Had these with Joshua been on Jordan's banks,
   They'd have been stoned, or hung as high as Haman.
In trade or war, when men commence to plunder,
Society and armies fall asunder.

But lest my reader, in his wisdom, should
   Carp at the views of this loose rambling letter,
Or that I, in my now excited mood,
   Should say things that, withheld, will less embitter,

I'll now trespass no longer, but conclude.
    Yet, by my stars, should trade not soon get
        better,
The members of the late commercial flash club
Must e'en be soused in my satiric wash tub.

Alack-a-day, that my impulsive muse
    Should for herself choose such ungracious subject,
Knowing, as she does well, the Press refuse
    Insertion to such samples of her budget.
Still, she cries out to propagate her views,
    And I unto her wayward whims am subject.
Vice to reprove, when Press and Pulpit scout it,
Who's left but Daunie Weir* and me to shout it?

---

    * A local peripatetic Demosthenes, still amongst us, who in his more vigorous years was wont to declaim with considerable shrewdness on popular grievances.

THE GO-A-HEADS.

WHY, when God's mercy has provided
   In barn and byre an ample store—
Enough to spread, if right divided,
   The family board of rich and poor—

That yet, despite this great profusion,
   The poor repine and cry for bread?
Why, simply from a cursed delusion,
   Called by the Yankees, "Go-a-head."

A-head of what? Commercial prudence?
   Our upstart merchants disarrange
By fraud, deceit, and bold impudence,
   The balance of trade's just exchange.

A-head of what? Commercial order?
   Men drive business everywhere,
O'er trade's legitimate safe border,
   Into speculation's snare.

With bland soft sawder, they deceive their
    Customers, and give them "tick,"
Who for a while, poor dupes, believe them
    Honest men, devoid of trick.

Their own accounts come due, and, hedging
    To clean out their somewhat empty till
To raise the needful, take to pledging
    Or forcing off goods—bring what they will.

Thus do the go-a-heads conjoin to
    Trade on stock that's not their own,
And order goods but to consign, to
    Raise another money loan.

Another mode of liquidating,
    Or squaring overdue accounts,
They find in bank accommodation,
    With cash at ruinous discounts.

Cash got—comes round the day of clearance
    With the Bank at four months' end;
The go-a-head makes his appearance,
    With some confidential friend

Who has some influence with the banker,
  Also, a fierce go-a-head;
The bill's renewed without a hanker,
  And all, by way of helping trade!

The go-a-heads thus play their gammon
  With the social weal of man,
And, by their zeal in serving mammon,
  Counteract the Gospel plan.

This lust for this unrighteous mammon
  Has snapt trade's spring and broke its wheel;
They ought to swing as high as Haman
  Who thus outrage the common weal.

This last expression I won't alter,
  Although it should grate on the ear;
It seems that nothing but a halter
  Will stop them in their mad career.

Man can live and not be selfish,
  Himself he can't enjoy alone;
His tastes resemble not the shell-fish,
  That lies beneath the sea-beach stone.

His very needs suggest communion :
If earthly comforts men require,
Efforts reciprocal and union
    Can only gain what they desire.

The Gospel precept—Love thy neighbour
    As thou wouldst thine own dear self—
Would add a blessing on man's labour,
    And guard against unrighteous pelf.

Down then with go-a-head chicanery,
    That brings trade to such awful pause,
Shutting up workshop, mill, and granary—
    God! help us to obey thy laws.

SABBATH MORNING REFLECTIONS.

ALL hail! thou ancient wood and glen—
  Gleniffer—here I come again,
    Thus early in the Spring,
To view each soul-inspiring scene,
And hear thy birds in merry strain
    Their Maker's praises sing.

Freed from the busy, swarming crowd
That seethe beneath yon smoky cloud
    That rises o'er each lum;
To enjoy the sweets of secret prayer,
And breathe the caller morning air,
    I early hither come.

O blest retreat, where, free from toil,
How pleasing 'tis to muse a while
    On that mysterious Power
Who formed this earth, these woods and glens,
These wild, romantic, rocky dens
    Adorned with many a flower.

Sure 'tis no crime on Sabbath morn,
Before the bells the people warn,
 To mount the hill of prayer;
To take a walk in sober mood,
And muse upon the Great and Good,
 Who's present everywhere.

No! thus removed from worldly strife
And all the busy cares of life,
 In this retired abode,
The soul in solemn converse sweet,
Soars, as it were on wings, to meet
 Its maker and its God.

TO THE MEMORY OF ALLAN STEWART.*

O SAY not, my friends, that young ALLAN is dead!
  It chills the warm blood in my veins!
For although the green turf now covers his head,
His spirit still hovers around, as we tread
  The scenes now endear'd by his strains.

His shade still does linger by Cart's winding stream,
  Where love's early passion he prov'd;
When "twilight's soft star on its bosom does beam,"
To lovers unborn, on its banks that may dream,
  He will whisper how dearly he lov'd.

"Down Inchinnan Loan," when the soft evening gale
  Is fraught with the scent of the " peas,"

---

* A young friend, the author of a posthumous volume of poems, published the year after his decease, which took place at Paisley, 12th November, 1837, when in his 26th year. The above tribute to his memory appears in the volume referred to. The respect of the two friends must have been mutual, Stewart, in one of his principal pieces referring to his companion as follows :—
    "such a love as thine,
  Congenial *Picken*, which doth here illume
  Life's darkest winter with eternal bloom."

On the zephyr's light wing his spirit does sail,
And echo is heard oft repeating the tale,
   Of his love 'neath the old Douglas trees.

"Thy banks, bonny Gryfe!" shall resound with
   his praise,
The scene of his childhood's fleet dream;
Young lovers that woo by the "breckan-bush braes,"
Will cherish his memory, and sing the sweet lays
   He gave to his dear native stream!

His voice is still heard in "Glenpatrick's" cool
   grove,
'Mid the soft hushing sound of the linn;
And his spirit still dwells in the bower which he
   wove
With sweet honeysuckle, to shelter his love,
   Afar from the town's stirring din.

Then say not, my friends, that young ALLAN is dead!
   It chills the warm blood in my veins!
For although the green turf now covers his head,
His spirit still hovers around, as we tread
   The scenes now endear'd by his strains!

EPISTLE TO A FRIEND.

NOW the wintry winds are blowing
   Bleak and cold athwart the lea,
And the streamlets cease from flowing
   Freely onwards to the sea :
Stern frost has stayed their onward glide,
And snow enwraps the green hill-side;
While all around the gazer's sight
Is an expanse of spotless white.

My muse, on days of pleasure dreaming,
   Sings its waefu' tale to thee,
While the tears are downward streaming,
   O'er hectic cheek from sorrowing e'e :
Yet, wherefore should these tears upstart,
Dragging deep sighs from my young heart ?
Had prudence led each step through life,
My sorrows had not been so rife.

But thou art blythe and happy too—
    Ah! thankfu' be that it is so;
Long may'st thou thrive, my ain dear Hugh,
    Each day may'st thou new pleasures know;
And may thy wife, so kind and free,
Be spared to share each joy wi' thee,—
From thy good deeds may blessings rise
That Heaven will own, nor earth despise.

Long may the favours of kind Heaven
    Keep thee and thine from sorrows free,
And may'st thou give as thou hast given,
    To such as need thy charity,—
May shrivelled poortith pass thy door,
    Want's shadow never on it rest,
And, may thy basket and thy store,
    Thine "oil and meal," be ever blest.

ON THE DEATH OF JANET PICKEN.

Who died 13th June, 1850.

DEPARTED one! forgive these selfish tears,
   Shed since thou left us and this world of woe;
Unmindful we that thou above the spheres
   Liv'st in such bliss as mortals here below
   Can only guess at. Still we hope to know
And taste with thee that bliss, when summoned hence
   From this to us now lonely, friendless, state;
We'll join thee in thy Heavenly residence,
   Where death nor grief shall ne'er disturb us more.
   Then will our souls again assimilate,
   As, ties renewed, together we adore
   The great Almighty, who did consummate
Our bliss by Mercy's plan;—then, too, unfurled,
We'll view the mysteries of that Better World.

TO A TRACT ABOUT TO BE POSTED TO A DISTANT FRIEND.

THOU little four-paged periodic tract,
 With wood-cut of a dove with olive branch descending,
I'll place another emblem* on thy back
 To waft thee on thy distant path, as wending
Thy way, by night and day, o'er land and sea,
Through city, township, wilderness, prairie,
 To where the links of civ'lised life are broken.
In loghouse, hut, or lonely shepherd's tent
 Thou'lt find my friend, and be to him a token
That, though our separation I lament,
 He's not of God nor yet of me forgotten;
 For sure thy page (with reverence be it spoken)
Points to God's grace and truth in every line—
Thy date refers to Paisley and langsyne.

---

* The postage stamp.

FAREWELL TO JAMES RONALD.*

WHILE winter lingers in our vales,
    And mingles March dust with his snaw,
The ship awaits propitious gales
    To bear our worthy guest awa';
We've met this night in Boyle's large ha',
    To bid farewell with loving hearts,
And pay him blythely, ane and a',
    The tribute due to his deserts.

Friend Ronald's individual worth,
    Although he strove to hide his name,
Has thus spontaneously called forth
    His friends' and townsmen's loud acclaim

---

* Mr. James Ronald, first as a designer and finally as a manufacturer, was long connected with our local shawl trade. One by one his near relations had settled in America, and, more in compliance with the wishes of his family than from any particular longings of his own, he resolved to follow. The valedictory meeting referred to in Mr. Picken's lines took place in the spring of 1851, immediately previous to Mr. Ronald's departure. Of liberal views in politics, Mr. Ronald had a strong love for democratic institutions, and particularly for the American form of government; but during a ten years'

In praise of him and those whose aim
Is to dethrone tyrannic might,
And gain, for all, the righteous claim
Which manhood has to Freedom's right.

Although he dwell in distant lands,
This tribute of respect and love
Will join us closer, heart and hands,
To give Reform another shove;
Till, in progression's onward move,
Tyrannic power is paralysed,
And, with God's blessing from above,
The people shall be enfranchised.

---

residence in Detroit, this became considerably modified, his blunt Scotch honesty causing him to speak out freely when dissatisfied. Ultimately he settled in Canada, its institutions and people proving in the end more in accordance with his likings. Having acquired a moderate competency, he eventually relinquished business, and visited the mother country more than once, During his last visit he had some thoughts of settling permanently at home, under the impression that his health would thereby be benefited; but his attachment to his family proved stronger than his wish to remain, and he returned to America. His death took place at Chatham, Ontario, on 22nd Dec., 1872, in his 64th year, in the midst of his much loved family circle.

TO THE MEMORY OF JAMES PICKEN,

Who died 9th Sept., 1857.

THOUGH dead, his memory still is wreathed
    Around our sorrowing hearts;
In garlands he himself bequeathed
    Ere from us he did part,
To join a sweet and happy band
Of friends in the mysterious land.

Why do we mourn when he is safe
    Within his Father's home?
Why do our hearts so keenly crave
    For pleasures not their own?
We, too, are pilgrims here below,
Throughout this world's changing show.

In life he was our stay and guide;
    His counsel and his smile,
When pressed with care on every side,
    Our fears did oft beguile,
And raised fresh hopes within our breast
That lulled our carking thoughts to rest.

In faith he lived, in faith he died,
    And left us here behind,
To mourn another severed tie
    Which time can never bind;
For, as its tide shall onward flow
We'll think on him while here below.

His absence now we keenly feel;
    'Tis trying to sustain;—
Tears down our cheeks oft trickling steal,
    Sure heralds of the pain
That, secret, lurks within our breast,—
Though unmarred is his peaceful rest.

Oh, when we meet! How we'll regain
    The friendship that is lost,
And, on sweet Canaan's radiant plain,
    Join with the ransomed host
In songs triumphant to our God,
Who gave us such a blest abode.

THE WEAVER'S CHILD.*

GOD help thee, child; with hardships soon
    Thou hast become acquaint;
Thy days did scarcely count a moon
When artificial tube and spoon
    Supplied thy only want.

God help thee, child! thy mother's sick,
    Her care thou must forego;
To lay upon her breast thy cheek,
And nestle there with lambish freak,
    Is bliss thou canst not know.

---

* The end of 1857 was one of those periodic periods of depression when the weavers of Paisley suffered considerably from want of employment. From a note attached to these verses in the *Renfrewshire Independent*, where they first appeared, we learn that upwards of a thousand decent tradesmen were at the time out of employment, and that a considerable portion of them were enduring all the miseries consequent on the loss of "daily bread." The verses in their manuscript state had been of service to the suffering poor, and were inserted by their author in the journal referred to in the hope that still greater results would follow, by their being read at the firesides and parlour tables of the more affluent class.

God help thee, child! thy father's poor;
    He cannot hire a nurse
To nourish thee and other four,
And thy sick mother; ah! 'tis more
    Than workman can disburse.

God help thee, child! the rich withhold
    The very crumbs of wealth;
They do not now, like Job of old,
Search out the cause of grief untold,
    And give relief by stealth.

God help thee, child! thy country's laws
    Exclude thee from the parish;
Unless th' Almighty God withdraws
Thy father's health like poor mamma's,
    They never will thee cherish.

God help thee, child, for Jesus' sake!—
    His bosom swelled with love
As little children he did take,
And thus to his disciples spake:
    "Of such is Heaven above."

STORIE STREET WELL.

SUNG BY THE AUTHOR, AT THE SOCIAL MEETING OF THE NATIVES
AND OLD RESIDENTERS OF STORIE STREET, HELD
16TH DECEMBER, 1853.

[The "Callans" of the various districts of Paisley have, during the last five-and-twenty years, held annual social re-unions of natives and residents of their respective localities, where gentle and semple meet on the terms of perfect equality they did in the olden days, when they "were boys together." In general these meetings are associated with some scheme of contributing, in the severities of the winter season, to the necessities of the aged and deserving poor, and many a humble fire has burned brighter in virtue of the well-considered kindnesses of these homely gatherings. On these occasions old reminiscences are freely brought up, old stories told, old jokes repeated; and it can be easily understood how these quaint and humorous lines, read by the author, were relished by the Storie Street Callans at their reunion of 16th December, 1853. Mr. Picken was a native of Storie Street, where his family resided, and to it through life he was warmly attached. The well, half-a-century ago, was quite an institution; the domestic water supply at that time was all carried from these spring wells, in the "stoups," of which every bien housewife had a pair. The pump being the private property of those who contributed to its upkeep, the handle in summer droughts was under chain and padlock. Each afternoon about five o'clock it was unlocked with an air of considerable importance by the custodiers of the keys. Long before the hour of opening, the stoups began to be placed, and sixty or seventy pairs might stand in rank and file for the purpose of being filled. Strict justice was done; the first comer was first served, till all were supplied, when the well was again locked up till next morning. "Lang James" and "Tam Houston" were two of the most notable amongst the worthies who took charge. The "Rope-a-ree close" and "Goosedubs" lay near the head of the street, and being at best inhabited by the "arabs" of the period, who were always ready for a chance without troubling themselves in the matter of pecuniary contribution, their denizens, when they did come down "like the wolf on the fold," met with unceremonious usage from Tam, and were sent by his ill-tongue in search of water to quarters where it was presumably still scarcer than even in Storie Street when the wants of the long line of applicants had been duly satisfied.]

Thou sweet, mnemonic, retrospective muse,
I know not if thou'rt classed amongst the Nine;
But Scotchmen, when they meet for blythe carouse,
Invoke thee by the name of "Auld Langsyne:"
So hand in hand we will together join,
And quaintly to the "Paisley Callans" tell
How lairds and tenants bravely did combine
To search for water in a deep sunk well,
Long ere the pipes were laid from sweet Gleniffer's dell.*

W1' drinking o' healths and pledging each toast,
 I've emptied my bottle, and now I'm almost
Inclined to think, it would perhaps be as well
To fill up a bumper from Storie Street Well.
Its pump stands erect and still runs strong and clear,
Despite of the efforts of auld Dr. Kerr; †
In a' the hail town scarce ane stands but itsel',
Sae famed is the water of Storie Street Well.

---

* *i. e.*, Long before the town was supplied by gravitation with water from the hillsides of Gleniffer.

† The great promoter of the Gravitation Water Scheme, and whose monument is one of the most conspicuous erections seen on entering our cemetery.

Since Gleniffer water was brought to the town,
Some say the pump's useless and should be ta'en
   down;
But their principal reason, I guess, is to sell
And fuddle the pump of the Storie Street Well.
Na, na, let it stand; it is still of some use,
E'en to those who would sell it; when drapping
   the booze
They kneel to its pump and say in to themsel'—
"It aye comes to water frae Storie Street Well."

Amang wells o' the town it aye bore the degree,
Of being the best for the making o' tea,
And our mothers, ye mind, did us aften compel
To tak' up the turn* at the Storie Street Well.
When water was scarce during summer's warm
   drouth,
The stoups stood in raws to lang James's† close-
   mouth;

---

  * The order of precedence secured by the placing of the
"stoups."

  † A Storie Street worthy, who resided near the present entrance to the Priorscroft Bowling Green.

And shifting their places caused many a gell,
Wi' the wives and the weans around Storie Street Well.

Thrawn-gabbed Tam Houston had charge o' its keys,
And like others in office got mair than his fees;
His private emoluments were valuabĕl,
For filling sly stoups at the Storie Street Well.
Frae the Rope-a-ree close, the Townhead and Goosedubs,
The Irish came down wi' their pots and their tubs;
Ill tongu'd Tammy Houston whiles damn'd them to h—l
Without a drap water frae Storie Street Well.

The householders held every year a franchise,
For appointing a board to get up the supplies;
And when business was done they'd adjourn the councĕl,
To some public house near the Storie Street Well.
The gill and the yill gave their humour the fang,
They bantered each other, they roared and they sang;

It would take a whole night a' the smart jokes
   to tell,
That were cracked at the meetings of Storie
   Street Well.

"Truth's hid in a well," as the auld proverb says;
But the Well Committees, to their credit and praise,
Had truth in their dealings and friendship as well,
In a' their transactions of Storie Street Well.
Now Storie Street neighbours, I hope that my sang
Has been of some service in helping to fang
And good feeling draw out from each breast's
   inmost cell,
As the pump draws the water frae Storie Street
   Well.

THE GHAIST O' STORIE STREET WELL.
A Rhyming Rhapsody.

[In the Spring of 1866, certain changes were made on the old pump, and among other things a Cattle Trough attached to it. All this was pure vandalism in the eyes of Mr. Picken, and he was wont to resent it as a piece of ill-timed and unwarrantable interference. He had too much of the poetic temperament to suffer the destruction, on any mere plea of practical utility, of what through long association had in his eyes become venerable. Some little glorification and presentation work, in the shape of "Gowden Specs" that took place in connection with the changes, fairly roused his ire and brought back even the ghost of "auld Tam Houston's self" to enable him to give expression to it.]

SPIRIT of the Water Spring,
    That wells up through each strata ring
Of limestone, sandstone, mineral, iron,
Oh do come up and tune my lyre, on
A theme I really fear I'll tire on:
'Tis sae ludicrously complex,
Wi' "Cattle Troughs" and "Gowden Specs,"
An' personal names I scarce may spell,
Which, seeing "Truth lies in a well,"
Had best be mentioned by yersel'.

Hush! for I hear a rumbling sound
Of something underneath the ground.

I see a hoary mist arising,—
Well, really this is most surprising.
Ha! there's a Ghost or Water Kelpie,
Come, as I rashly prayed, to help me.

No, no! 'tis neither Ghost nor Elf,
But simply auld Tam Houston's self.
Stand back, ye youngsters,—swing nor jump
Nor play at leap-frog o'er the pump,
Or else, as he was wont, I'm thinking,
Auld Tam 'll gie your lugs a clinking,
An' gar ye quat your fun and jinking.
For there he stan's, as I hae min',
In the same claise he wore langsyne,—
Green worset apron, tied wi' string;
Blue bonnet, wi' a checkered ring;
His braces o'er his breeks hing slack,—
See, ane is dangling at his back,
His stockings slobber o'er his kuites,*
Shod wi' a pair of bauchelled† boots.
Whilst—ludicrous and strange phisog—
His mouth is thrawn maist to his lug!

---

* Ancles.   † Down in the heel.

(A warning taught our early youth,
That horrid swearing thrawed his mouth.)

Dear me! thae speerits o' the deed
Maun travel at a wondrous speed,
For, in the lan' abune the well,
Whar Tam langsyne abode himsel',
He's noo strong at his ill-tongued jeering;
An', as I am within the hearing,
I'll note it down—without the sweering.

"By a' that's guid," Tam loudly sweers,
"I'll ring your misdeeds in your ears.
What richt had ye, for ony spree,
To bring this turmoil upon me?
An', for mere praise unto yersel',
Pretend that ye've improved the well?
I hae a mind to vex and teaze ye,
Till ye see self as ithers see ye.
Great need, indeed, o' mental specs
Hae ye to see yer ain defecs!
For praise you've really sich an itching,
You couldna see your friends were bitching
Whan they gied you thae pinchbeck specs
In token o' their warm respecs

For you, anent your late connection
With that great jaw-box trough erection.
But e'en for this I wadna cared
That 'bacca spittle o'er my beard,
Had you no sent unto the papers
A flash report o' a' your capers,
Bringing my old loved well to shame,
And a' connected wi' its name.
For this, atonement must be made
By printing every word I've said
In the next issue of the press;
And if I don't get this redress,
By Jove—by everything that's dear—
I'll hae't proclaimed by Daunie Weir!"

I heard nor saw nae mair o' Tam;
He gaed awa', swift as he cam',
In flaming rage at the presumption
And impudent and rash assumption
Of interlopers, weak and vain,
On his old cherished dear domain;
But satisfied, beyond a doubt,
For ance he'd fairly spoken out,
An' tauld the meddlers to their face,
O' his ain dear auld well's disgrace.

FRAGMENT
OF AN EPISTLE TO A FRIEND.

YOU ask me oft why I come down?
    The reason why I'll frankly own;
For sure it is a pleasant task
For me to grant what you may ask;
Then take my answer, strong in rhyme,
It's true at least, if not sublime,—
Void of that wit which makes a poet;
But what it has I'm proud to show it.

Bards meantime are by no means scanty—
I wish potatoes were as plenty,
We then might roast an average crop,
And for our living have some hope;
But webs, and "duffs,"* and coals are scarce
And nothing plentiful, but—verse.

In every lane you'll find a score
Who verses write—you've read before—

---

* "Duffs," "spuds"—colloquials for "potatoes."

If they, by favour, can bespatter
A corner of the *Liberator*,*
They deem their head a golden mint,
Though lead's the only ore that's in't.
Their lines are like a worsted clout,
No sooner lichted than it's out—
When all is dark as their own ink,
And nought remains,—but smoke and stink!

I know a spouting tap-room sot,
Had he but sense and learning got,
And a bold theme to build his fire on,
He thinks he'd far eclipse Lord Byron.
But poverty, the beldam slee,
Has locked his brains and lost the key!
Perhaps 'tis well such fate prevails,
Else who could work for reading tales;
And here am I, without one verse
The twentieth century will rehearse,
Daring to wish that Madame Fame
Will not o'erlook my handsome name,

---

* A newspaper of extreme Liberal politics, published in Glasgow about and after the Reform Bill agitation of 1831-2-3.

But hand it down to future times—
A meteor stuck above my rhymes;
And, more than that, O madly vain!
I've wished the volume would contain,—
What would you think? I blush to tell,—
A likeness o' my bonnie sel'!

Unless fair genius show her smile,
A wish for fame's a reptile vile
That drain's the sap from reason's root,
And leaves proud man a speaking brute.
We tug our brains, scratch heads, and toil,
As if lamps could burn withouten oil.

THE MARTYRS' GRAVE.*

OUR heath-clad hills and mountain caves
    Are mark'd by battle-fields and Martyrs' graves.
This stone records the last embattled stroke
Which Scotchmen struck at vile Oppression's yoke.
At BONNYMUIR they trod their native heath,
And sought a Warrior's or a Martyr's death.
Sad choice! for there they found their enterprise
To force or claim Reform by armed surprise
Was circumvented and betrayed by spies;
And thus ensnared in Treason's feudal laws,
Their personal honour in the people's cause
Compelled the fight which claims our pity and applause.

---

* These lines were written as an inscription for the monument erected in Paisley Cemetery in 1867, in honour of the memories of Andrew Hardie and John Baird, who were executed for high treason in 1820. Young and zealous, these men took an active part in the political agitations of 1819–20, which, there is too much reason to believe, were fostered and encouraged by spies in the pay of Government. What would now be regarded as little more than breaches of the peace

were then construed into "compassing the death of the King"; and the unfortunate march of James Wilson of Strathaven, with a few enthusiasts like himself, in the direction of Glasgow, the stopping of certain mills at Johnstone through the influence of James Speirs and others, and the armed resistance of Baird, Hardie, and their companions, at Bonnymuir, near Stirling, to a troop of yeomanry who had been sent out to disperse them, ended alike disastrously. James Wilson was executed at Glasgow, 30th August, 1820; Baird and Hardie at Stirling, on Sept. 8; while James Speirs, tried at Paisley on 1st and 2nd August of the same year, was only saved by the impossibility of securing a unanimous verdict, rendered necessary by the English statute, under which the Government, to increase the chances of conviction, resolved to try him. The Radical weavers of Paisley necessarily sympathised with the objects of Government persecution, and to this day cherish the memories of Baird and Hardie, as martyrs in the highest sense of the term. Hence the monument in question, and Mr. Picken's noble inscription.

ELEGY ON WALTER PEACOCK,*

Town's Drummer in Paisley.

MOURN a' ye folks in Paisley toun,
    An' in its suburbs roun' and roun',
For Wattie Pea'ock's past the gloom
    O' Death's dark shade;
An' noo he sleeps fu' fast an' soon
    Amang the dead.

Hech, friens, hoo Time doth alter things!
He baith new folk an' fashions brings,
An' sweeps awa' wi' brushing wings
    Baith laigh an' high,
E'en wha'd refresh our memory's springs
    Wi' things gane by.

---

* Walter Peacock was town drummer and ringer of the bell of the Cross Steeple upwards of twenty years, but he was better known by the name of "Wattie Paik." He had a *hersheugh* lip, and consequently was a bad speaker; and, being of an irritable temper, he was tormented by boys knocking on his drum when he had it shouldered, and mocking his speech. He died about 1830.

Since noo "Fire Rab"* an' Wattie's gane,
An' Johnny Lusk's to Poors-House ta'en,†
About the Cross, alack there's nane
    O' ancient folk,
Except "Peastrae"‡ standing alane
    At Weir's book-shop. §

It's but shortsyne since I began
To watch the brief career o' man;

---

* Robert Hart, weaver and fireman, better known by the name of "Fire Rab" and "Fire in the Linwood," resided in the Townhead of Paisley. The greatest fire he ever attended was the burning of the Linwood Cotton Mill, which happened on Friday, the 20th of November, 1801, when the mill was burned to the ground. He was late in hearing of it, and ran out the whole road—2½ miles—bawling "Fire in the Linwood and me no there." In going to other fires afterwards, he frequently roared at the height of his voice, "Fire in the Linwood." Rab died in 1827.

† John Lusk, tailor, Townhead, was called "Wee Johnnie Lusk." His name appears in the Directory for 1810. He was an innocent body, and would not work, but lounged about the flesh market. After his father's death he was taken into the Town's Hospital, where he died.

‡ Robert Smith, well known by the *soubriquet* of "Peastrae," was a book auctioneer in Orr Square. He died in 1845, aged eighty years.

§ John Weir, bookseller, 104 Cross. He died about 1828.

But through an' through I aye hae fan'
    It was the case
That as ane died, anither cam'
    To fill his place.

But still it brings some smarting pain
To those wha're in the musing strain,
To pairt wi' them they thocht their ain
    By wont and use,—
Although, while here they did remain,
    They got abuse.

I mind hoo, wi' a teasing train
O' bairns, I'd after Wattie gane,
An' at his drum whiles flung a stane
    To gar it soun',
Whan wi' his sticks he'd chase us hame
    Wi' crunted croon.

I mind, too, aften at the "drawing," *
Whan I at nicht asleep was fa'ing,

---

* The occupation of the great bulk of Paisley boys in the first forty years of the century,—the "draw-boy" being an indispensable assistant at the harness-loom. The jacquard machine has, however, during the last thirty years, so increased

O' being cheered to hear the ca'ing
  O' Wattie's bell;
But noo, alas! he's paid his lawing
  An' sleeps himsel'.

An' whan, at rare times it befel,
He'd booze till he forgat himsel,
An' miss the ringing o' his bell
  At ten o'clock,
Faith mony mair beside mysel'
  He did provoke.

For then oor maisters, on the "push," *
Would never speir hoo hours did rush,
But wi' the wark would drive and brush
  Wi' bickerin speed;
Whilst worn and tired we'd aften wish
  That they were dead.

---

in use, as to make the draw-boy a thing of the past. The draw-boy had to be at his master's call at all hours, early and late; and no doubt when ten o'clock arrived, he, tired and sleepy, was cheered indeed
  "To hear the ca'ing o' Wattie's bell."

* The master weaver working too often by fits and starts, was frequently, at week-ends especially, on the "push," making up for lost time.

Puir Watty! twenty years an' mair
The bell an' drum were in his care;
An', noo his dead, it's only fair
    For us to say
He did—richt weel—what to his share
    Fell in his day.

ALAS! THEY'RE GONE WHO CHEERED ME.

I FIGHT an aimless battle
    With this world's tittle tattle,
But no ray of hope or pleasure lights the way;
    For they are gone who cheered me,
    Though some are left who please me;
But soon, too, I must follow on the way.

In my days of youthful pleasure,
    I never dreamt—ah, never!—
That my joys thus would wither and decay;
    For though tried friends are near me,
    - Who by acts of love oft cheer me,
Still, the old remembered faces are away.

ON READING A BURLESQUE SERMON TO BACHELORS.

"The course of true love never did run smooth."
—*Shakspeare.*

THIS mimic preacher would have men to woo
    As doth a tom-cat on a barn or stable;
When maukins will not listen to his mew
    He leaps right through the bole-hole of the gable,
And there shrieks out another yello-hoo
    In hopes to fascinate some other female,
Caring not whether she be black or white,
Provided she but condescends to bite.

With most men, wooing's quite another thing—
    Their amours are not just so migratory:
The impression of an early love will cling
    Unto their heart until their head grows hoary.
Nay, many instances I could easily bring,
    Alike from ancient and from modern story,
Of dying men who even spoke with gladness
Of meeting soon the cause of their long earthly
    sadness.

A LIGHT TO LIGHTEN THOSE WHO LEAPT INTO POLITICAL DARKNESS.

WHEN Whig and Tory, for reform,
    Arranged the household mark,
Each party swithered to perform
    The "leap into the dark." *

Since then. Bill Gladstone's led the way,†
    And has been very busy,
Reducing Church and State outlay,
    Despite of Mr. Dizzy.

But since the Franco-Prussian war,
    The Tories, apprehensive

---

* Mr. Disraeli's outbidding of Mr. Gladstone, by extending the suffrage to householders while his rival had proposed only a £7 rental qualification, took the breath alike from Whig and Tory, and was well named "a leap in the dark." *

† Mr. Gladstone, in virtue of the sweeping majority of Whig members returned under the extended suffrage, replaced Mr. Disraeli in office before the meeting of the New Parliament,—the latter having seen the hopelessness of meeting, as Prime Minister, the Parliament of his own creation. During the succeeding five years Mr. Gladstone was indeed "very,"—perhaps overly,—"busy."

That our neutrality might jar
With movements so extensive,

Got up the outcry in their need—
"Increase our coast defences,"
Which made our outlay far exceed
A prudent year's expenses.

Then came the proof of the remark
On the enlarged franchise;
Each party groping in the dark
To find new tax supplies.

The Exchequer struck a *match-box spark*,*
From which a light did rise,
Of *burning words* spoke in Hyde Park,†
Which opened all their eyes.

Both parties now may plainly see
The truth, 'twill hide no longer,

---

* Mr. Lowe's proposal to tax lucifer matches.

† The populace, it will be remembered, held monster meetings in Hyde Park, and literally spoke burning words on this occasion.

Of Byron's bird-sung prophecy—
  "The people are the stronger."

Taxation's burden now must be
  Laid equal on each class;
For working-men will not woo-gee,
  And bear it like an ass.

The landed aristocracy
  Must learn proportion's rule;
Also, some lessons in the *Free*
  Commercial Reading School,

That they may comprehend more clear
  Taxation's Indicator,—
A book revised every year
  By one called *Valuator.*

May, 1871.

SCHOOL BOARD ELECTIONS AND COMIC CARTOONS.*

(APRIL, 1873.)

IN the heat of the School Board elections,
  Cartoons, with a comic grimace,
Burlesqued the dear old Scottish questions
  Concerning the doctrines of grace.

The artist referred to "foreknowledge,"
  An attribute purely divine,—
The learning of no school or college
  Can grasp the Almighty design.

They may laugh, they may jeer, they may pun,
  And for false explanations may look;

---

* In the first election to the School Boards, in April, 1873, an intense amount of excitement was manifested on the question of Bible and Catechism teaching in the new schools; and, feeling running high, the satire of those opposed to Bible and Catechism occasionally bordered on the irreverent. In Paisley, one or two cartoons exhibited gave as much evidence of wit as of wisdom, and shocked the better sense of the seriously-minded. Mr. Picken, attached to the good old ways, and especially to the "Old Question Book," was evidently troubled at any burlesquing of "dear old Scottish questions concerning the doctrines of grace."

But of modern productions, not one
    Can compare with the Old Question Book.

This election, with pencil-mark crosses, *
    Will serve to illustrate the case,—
Nine only can win, while ten loses; †
    Yet each candidate works for a place.

Some parties may guess and surmise,
    Split their votes, or bestow them in plump, ‡
But the truth still is hid from their eyes,
    Till officially added in slump.

Time is up!—all the boxes are sealed,—
    The Board is already elected;

---

* Each voter marked on the Ballot slips, with a pencil-cross, the names he or she selected.

† Nineteen candidates stood for the nine vacancies.

‡ The cumulative vote being allowed under the Education Act, each voter could give one or more votes, up to nine, and these could be concentrated on one candidate, or split over as many as was considered desirable. Some of the candidates returned by the largest number of votes had the smallest number of voters, these having *plumped*, or given their entire nine votes to their favourite, so that his election might be made secure. Less partizan voters *split* or divided their votes over the candidates akin to them in sentiment.

Of the nineteen names therein concealed
   Nine are chosen, and ten are rejected.

The ballot, in darkness and doubt,
   Veils our senses from aiding our reason,—
A precarious practice throughout,
   Tempting Emperors and tyrants to treason.*

But the gospel election is free,
   Without even the shade of a doubt,—
The call is, "Who cometh to me
   I'll in no way reject or cast out."

Things earthly we misapprehend,
   When our bodily senses are blinded;
But by prayer heavenly things recommend
   Themselves to the heavenly-minded.

Our redemption is bought with a price,
   And sealed by Christ's blood on the cross,
And the grand covenanted invoice
   Has no margin of probable loss.

---

* A reference, probably, to the plebiscites of Napoleon III.

From sin's curse, God in Christ sets us free;
   Constrained by his love, we love others,
And this is assurance that we
   Are adopted God's sons and Christ's brothers.

FRAGMENT.

Dear S——, thou oft remindst me of
   A beauteous bed of flowers,
Grown wild for want of culture's hand
   To guide its spreading powers.

Were education but bestowed
   Upon thy fertile mind,
The flowers which nature planted there
   Would blossom more refined.

THE SCHOOL BOARD AND THE DRILL HALL INDIGNATION MEETING.*

WHILE standing at the Cross the other day,
    With other idle† weavers, idly talking,
Merely to wile the tedious hours away
    (The equinoctial gales prevented walking),
One subject of our varied colloquy
    Gave rise to thoughts which I've thought worthy chalking
Down into rhyme; for I can't check or bridle
My town-bred muse when I am going idle.

Lest some should deem my verses stark mad prose,
    I will, with two-three words of explanation,
Shortly my heart-felt inward thoughts disclose,
    Touching this scheme of National Education,

---

* A public meeting held in the Drill Hall, 16th Sept., 1874, to remonstrate against the proposed School Rate, and the extravagant ideas, as the promoters held it, of the School Board in regard to buildings.

† A local term for want of employment.

And of the conduct of such as oppose
  Our local School Board's wise administration.
Fie! Paisley, fie! the first to give annoyance
  To modern, broad, sound, views of Social Science.

Daughters and sons of Paisley, by your votes
  You chose nine men to set your schools agoing;
They made the philanthropic THOMAS COATS
  Their chairman, thereby to you plainly showing,—
Although your voting was like casting lots,—*
  You had got men whose hearts were warmly
    glowing
With the desire to elevate the masses,
And healthy school-room give to all the varied
  classes.

Grant that the School Board's plan for space
    exceeds
  The strict requirements of the legislative
    measure,
What then? The Chairman to his noble deeds
  Adds yet another from his personal treasure:

---

* *i. e.*, by ballot.

Give but the children what he thinks their needs,
He'll pay the extras with good-will and pleasure.
Actions like this mankind delight to honour;
Men yet unborn will bless this worthy donor.*

Like the Apostle Paul, I may exclaim—
    Oh, foolish working men! Who hath bewitched you
To crowd the Drill Hall thus, and join acclaim
    With cunning ones who'd, by their logic, teach you
To think your interest and theirs the same?—
    Because they need your help they thus beseech you
To join them in their sordid indignation
And their ill-judged, unpatriotic deputation. †

---

* Mr. COATS, anxious to give the maximum amount of air and space in the new schools to the children, without unduly alarming the economical narrowness that had been manifested by the promoters of the Drill Hall meeting, generously offered to personally meet all the extra cost that would be incurred over that of complying with the strict requirements of the statute. An offer involving a probable gift of from £4000 to £5000.

† The deputation sent to the Central Board, at Edinburgh, to prevent, if possible, the adoption of the building

Workmen! for your dear children's sake be wise;
    For them you are in duty bound to labour;
If you receive your labour's proper prize,
    Then pay the school-rates with your richer neighbour:
For children's sake use wisely the franchise,
    The Act is altogether in their favour.
If you can't pay the rates, the parish must.
For Labour, thus, the Schools are held in trust.

If selfish men oppress the labouring poor,
    And render them unfit to do their duty,
This Education measure points a cure,
    The law of which is full of heavenly beauty.
In the school-rate, oppressors must restore
    Us back a portion of extorted booty.
More laws like this would lead men to enquire
Who pays, and who pays not, for Labour's hire.

    October, 1874.

---

plans adopted by the local board. The plans having been in the end duly sanctioned, the spirit of contention rapidly died away.

THE TANNAHILL CENTENARY,

3RD JUNE, 1874.

This fragment,—the last lines written by Mr. Picken,—forms but the commencement of what might have been a poem of some length. The verses have been printed from the first draftings in pencil—in which there is little evidence of their having undergone much revision or correction at his hand.

O LEAVE me not, my quaint, descriptive Muse,
    Before we part we'll wander up the hill,
And, in some bushy, cozie den, peruse
    The published record of our Tannahill
    Centenary. 'Twill make my bosom thrill
With the warm glow of brighter, younger years;
    For now I'm old, and could not press uphill
To join the throng and hear their joyous cheers,
That Tannahill's sweet songs have stood the test
    of years.

Aye, Tannahill! thy beautiful word-pictures,
    Wed to the lyre by the musician's art
On memory's leaves, are photographic fixtures

That form an album in a Scotsman's heart;
And should he from his native home depart,
Following life's fortunes, or by land or sea,
His youthful loves and sylvan walks will start
As thrilling echoes of sweet memorie
At the soft notes o' "Bonnie Craigielea."

The maiden of his early love, who 'mong
Her friends and kindred waits for his return,
Finds, too, a solace in thy gushing song,
And sings "Langsyne, beside the woodland burn;"
Or, should her thoughts take still another turn,
And muse on wintry scenes round "Stanley shaw,"
Where songless birds on leafless twigs but mourn
Or chirp and flutter 'mongst the drifting snaw,
She pities them, and thinks on him that's "far awa'."

And should they meet beside the "Dusky Glen,"
Or climb, in thought, "Glenkilloch's sunny brae,"
They recognise each rocky, foggy den
With "feathery breckans" hung, wherein they lay
Langsyne, to shun the gowden, sunny, ray.

Returning home, they pass the "birken shaw,"
   Its rose suggests sweet talk,—they name the day,
Heedless alike of " cankert minnie's " say;
Aye, though their bridal bed should be " o' clean
      pea-strae."

But stop, my muse! We're on a dangerous path;
   His doric muse to alter or construe,
I fear, may only make my reader laugh,
   And say that really I've writ nothing new:
   When I began, the theme I had in view
Was to describe the Tannahill ovation,
   So by thy leave we'll make the start anew,
And write a short sketch of the demonstration,
Ending, it may be, with some gaudy peroration.

The morning star does scarcely usher in
   This third June morning's dawn on Paisley town,
When young and old, with joyous hearts, begin
   To honour her who wears our royal crown,
   And him who gave to us a new renown.
A mutual tribute this to Queen and Bard,[*]

---

[*] The local celebration of Her Majesty's birth-day was fixed for 3rd June—the centenary of Tannahill—to avoid the necessity of two holidays coming too close together.

To him of whom the critics freely own
His songs have earned the minstrels' proud reward,
Their country's favour, and their Queen's regard.

Why thus connect his hundredth natal day
    And fifty-fifth of our beloved Queen?
The reason is, to make one holiday
    Out of two halves, with scarce a week between.
    A brighter sunny day is rarely seen;
The people in their holiday attire,
    To music's march, in companies convene,—
Love, loyalty, and song, their breasts inspire,
To form with Nature's self a most harmonious
    choir.

Paisley, indeed, is nicely decked this morn
    With floral arches, interspersed with green,
And everywhere the smile of pride is borne
    Upon each face. Each actor on the scene,—
    The hoary head, or youth of scarce eighteen,—
Wears the same happy smile, devoid of scorn.
    Old "Seestu's" sons and daughters both, I ween,

Are emulous of each other, to adorn
And "leafify" the town where Tannahill was born.

. . . . . .

Sweet Bard, thy songs alike may cheer the heart
    Of strolling beggar or of titled squire;
Upon life's stage thou nobly didst thy part,
    Till reason left thee, and thou didst expire,
    Thy worth unknown. But, as the smouldering fire
That burns unseen, bursts out into a glow,
    So bursts thy fame,—which men at length desire
To honour,—and, that all the world may know
Of their regard, have framed this proud imposing show.

. . . . . .

FREE BREAKFASTS AND BONDED LIGHTS.

[Written on Mr. Lowe's famous attempt to impose a tax on lucifer matches, which collapsed before the floods of opposition and raillery with which it was assailed. The cry for a Free Breakfast table Mr. Picken held inconsistent with the attempt to tax the match that lit the morning fire.]

"FREE breakfasts to the working man!"—
    John Bull doth growl and mutter,—
"Free breakfasts; bait me if you can
    With untaxed bread and butter!
What! tax the very match's flame
With which I lit my fire? Oh, shame
Upon such Low(e) cave-born* finesse
As tries to make our humble comforts less."

April, 1871.

---

* In allusion to the "Cave of Adullam,"—the master stroke of sarcasm which Mr. Bright applied to Mr. Lowe and his party regarding their conduct on the Reform Bill of 1868.

WHIGS AND TORIES.

A. D. 1839.

ALTHOUGH the Tories noo are gone,
   Wi' a' their base intrigues,
The Radicals maun still anon
   Be wary o' the Whigs.
The battle noo is but begun,
   Though we the "Bill" ha'e got,
An' whether we're to lose or win
   Depends on how we vote.

We can o' Whigs an' Tories trace
   Nae difference but in name;
They baith are bent on power and place,
   Their creeds are much the same.
In power, the Whigs are Tories then,
   The Tories they are Whigs—
I've said, and frankly say't again,
   "They're a' the same sow's pigs."

We thought, if Whigs got into power,
   That Britain would be free;

At all events, we might be sure
    A mighty change to see.
'Bout things they used to roar against
    They never noo play cheep,
And feint a hait to us restore
    But what they canna keep.

"Monopolies" nae mair engage;
    "The Debt" they never heed;
Baith "Universal Suffrage"
    An' "Vote by Ballot"'s dead.
O' "Annual Parliaments" nae mair
    We hear a single word,
And mony a thing is noo deemed fair
    That ance appeared absurd.

Then send baith Whigs and Tories hence;
    Employ anither sort,—
Frae 'mang oursel's choose men o' sense,
    Though we should them support—
Men who will neither "gee" nor "gwine"—
    Reformers to the bone,
Pledged to the teeth to tell our min'
    In a determined tone.

Then follow ye what I advise,
  An' soon the day will come,
Whan we'll our Whigs an' Tories rise,
  An' gar them baith sing dumb.
I trust we'll gie posterity
  The pleasant tale to tell,—
We sent the Whigs to Purgatory,
  The Tories to—ah! well.

TOM HOOD IN A FIX.

An Impromptu for the Club.

THE droll Tom Hood, the other week,
Tells us his fancy took a freak,
Amid the fumes of toddy reek
    In his own dwelling,
To find out whiskey's name in Greek,
    But failed in spelling.

Should he come short in qualitie,
As thus in etymologie,
We'd have him come down here and see,
    By bead or measure,
Nae liquor e'er can bear the gree
    Wi' *Peter's* treasure.*

1873.

---

* The landlord's best.

THE NEW YEAR EXPECTANT.

CLICK, click, goes the clock
    Through these quiet nocturnal hours;
I will rise and take a smoke,
    And look its index, by the powers
Of this little Congreve light:
Hah! that dogged silent wight,
    Old Time's railway stoker,
    Has been driving with his poker
In a most unusual way.
    Faith he's passed the New Year station
    Whilst I've slept off the libation
That I drank on Hogmanay.

TO SANCT CRISPIN.

MY wants are so great that I really am scant
    E'en for bauchels to cover my cloots;
Do therefore insist on your men, Mr. Sanct,
    To make haste with my pair of new boots.

FRAGMENT.

"O DEAR, what a slop!
    Husband, I see you're still tipsy."
"I haven't, my dear, ta'en a drop
    This same blessèd year of that whisky."
"Had you staid in bed all the day,
We had not had this hubbub affray."
    "Your personal allusion
    Is quite a wrong conclusion.
This morning,—d' ye see,—
    It was my destiny to get up;
    I had no thought of this kick up;
It was—it was—involuntary!"

SONGS.

THE GALLANT PAISLEY WEAVER.*

Tune—"Weavers' March."

"Where Cart rins rowin' to the sea,
By many a flower and spreading tree,
There lives a lad, the lad for me,
And he's a gallant weaver."

THUS Robin Burns did sing the praise
   O' Paisley weavers in his days;
Unless they had deserved his lays
   He ne'er had sung o' weavers.

Burns tells us, too, I maun remark,
That strappin' Nannie's cutty sark
(The lass that chas'd Tam in the dark)
   Cam' frae the Paisley weavers.

---

* The Paisley weavers, like other trades, indulged for several years in an annual excursion by rail or river. On the occasion of their third annual excursion, their pilgri-

And since they wove that sark o' harn,
They've wrocht a' sorts o' waft and yarn—
Nocht comes amiss to han' or brain
    O' clever Paisley weavers.

Of weaving silk they learned the knack—
Baith plain and figured they did mak;
Sae rich in texture, ilk ane spak
    In praise o' Paisley weavers.

And then cam' in the cotton trade,
The finest muslin e'er was made,
And rich full harness flower'd brocade,
    Were wrocht by Paisley weavers.

The Indiana woollen plaid,
In a' the checks Scots clans supplied,
An' tartan dresses short an' side,
    Are wrocht by Paisley weavers.

---

mage was to the Land of Burns, the number of passengers on the occasion numbering about 1800. The day is recorded to have been one of sunshine and brilliance, and everything went off satisfactorily. The above song was Mr. Picken's contribution to the enjoyment of the day.

The richest dress worn at a ball,
The Queen's and Madame Kossuth's* shawl,
Whate'er the ladies " fancy " call,
    Is wrocht by Paisley weavers.

But if my hearers think this strain
O' panegyric rather vain,
Excuse me, for I'm in a train
    Wi' near twa thousan' weavers.

Forbye, I've got a gey bit tift
O' guid Scotch drink, whilk tends to lift
Some ither folk abune their height
    As weel's a Paisley weaver.

And 'twas a spirit-stirring scene
To whilk we short syne bade gude e'en,
The sacred fane o' our auld frien'
    That sang o' Paisley weavers.

---

* The lady of Louis Kossuth, the Hungarian patriot, was presented with a choice specimen of the Paisley Shawl, by the united weavers.

Their praises langer I micht sing,
But here my Jeanie, winsome thing,
Has gien my shouther a bit ding,
    An' whispered " quat your havers!"

WHEN YOU AND I, JEANNIE.

WHEN you and I, Jeannie, were wee things thegither,
  Doon by the burn-side we aften did stray;
An' walked hand in hand like a sister and brither,
  An' pu'd the sweet wild flowers that grew by the way.

An' while that you gathered the primrose and violet
  That grew 'mang the grass 'neath the wide spreading thorn,
I o'er in the wild wood did search for each floweret
  I thought was most worthy thy breast to adorn.

Ah, few were my cares in those days of my childhood,
  Compared with the many that now load my breast;
Nae mair will we seek our sweet flowers in the wild wood,
  Nae mair will I ever again feel so blest.

WAE'S ME!

LOSH me, ye are blest an' ken naething ava,
    Ye ha'e got a gudeman an' a house stocked
        fu' braw;
But though I've aye dune, an' still dae what I can,
I ha'e ne'er had the luck yet to get a gudeman.
                    Wae's me!

I crack weel wi' a' the auld lads that I ken—
But deed they're no lads noo, they're sensible men—
I coax them an' flatter as weel as I can,
An' ha'e dune an' said a', but "Come o' be my man."
                    Wae's me!

Ye'll think maybe I'm joking; hech, sirs, no ava,
For I've stept o'er the borders o' twa score an' twa;
Keep your thumb on that, Liz, for it may be I'm
        wrang—
There are aulder than me that ha'e gotten a man.
                    Wae's me!

Gi'e me the same chance as I had years gane by,
Like a cock at a grossart, I'll snap at the fly;
But Lizzie, my lass, could you no draw a plan
That would airt me at ance tae a canny gudeman.
Wae's me!

But don't say a word to my auld cronie, Nell,
For she's aulder than me, that ye ken weel yoursel';
Let us min' our ain han' an' plan weel our plan,
An' wha kens how sune I may get a gudeman.
Wae's me!

"HEART'S-EASE."

NOW, Ladies, when you sail,
    By steamboat or by rail,
Do not sigh so and bewail
    At a piteous mischance,—
Such as some one treading down
The crinoline of your gown;
Oh, do not call him clown!
    Rather give a favouring glance;
Resolve to be serene and pleased
    Wherever you may go,
Even though the creature comforts
    Should be,—ah, well! so, so.
Your smiles incite the gentlemen
    To do their best to please,
And add, as brawly ye a' ken,
    Unto your ain "Heart's-ease."

Dear Creatures, when you meet,
In drawing-room or street,
A gent not quite complete
    In the etiquette of France,

Do not spoil your face by frown,
Enough to knock him down;
Such deeds you must disown
    If your aims are to entrance.
Take all things in good part—
    Even when you can't agree;
For thus you'll gain the heart
    Of the gentlemen you see.
They all will then admire,
    And do their best to please,
Which adds, as brawly ye a' ken,
    Unto your ain "Heart's-ease."

And, Gentlemen, be smart,
For you know it is your part
To be on the alert,
    To serve each lady fair;
If a seat you can command,
When you see a lady stand,
Just take her by the hand
    And bow her to a chair.
Attend thus to the ladies,
    Wherever you may go—
Your mother, or your sister,

Or your lady-love—ho! ho!
Aye do the best you can,
    Each damsel fair to please,
'Twill ever bring its own reward
    In your ain "Heart's-ease."

Then, Gentlemen, attend;—
You the ladies must defend,
'Tis on you that they depend;
    Dare any one say No?
Though you find not one so meek
As your inward fancies seek,
Oh, never wet her cheek
    By causing tear to flow.
Far rather win a smile
    From the sweet lips of the fair;
And mind, in ancient style,
    It takes two to make a pair.
By bearing this in mind,
    You're always sure to please,
And be ever adding to the stock
    Of your ain "Heart's-ease."

THE END.

www.ingramcontent.com/pod-product-compliance
Lightning Source LLC
Chambersburg PA
CBHW020138170426
43199CB00010B/803